Dan Marino

Record-Setting Quarterback

SPORTS GREATS

by
Thomas S. Owens

The Rosen Publishing Group's
PowerKids Press™
New York

Published in 1997 by The Rosen Publishing Group, Inc.
29 East 21st Street, New York, NY 10010

First Edition

Book Design: Kim Sonsky

Photo Credits: Cover, pp. 15, 16 © Archive Photos; pp. 4, 7, 8, 10, 11, 19 © AP/Wide World Photos; p. 6 © Barry Elz/International Stock; p. 12 © Mike Valeri/FPG International; p. 14 © FPG International; p. 20 © Richard Mackson/FPG International.

Owens, Tom, 1960–
    Dan Marino : record-setting quarterback / Thomas. S. Owens.
       p.   cm. — (Sports greats)
    Includes index.
    Summary: Describes the life and career of the Miami Dolphins' star quarterback, who has broken more than twenty-five NFL records.
    ISBN 0-8239-5092-1
    1. Marino, Dan, 1961– —Juvenile literature. 2. Football players—United States—Biography—Juvenile literature. 3. Quarterback (Football)—Juvenile literature. 4. Miami Dolphins (Football team)—Juvenile literature. [1. Marino, Dan, 1961– . 2. Football players.] I. Title. II. Series: Sports greats (New York, NY)
    GV939.M29094 1997
    796.332'092—dc21
                                  97-4152
                                  CIP
                                  AC

Manufactured in the United States of America

Contents

Making Records

He licks his fingers, flings his strong right arm, then—ZAP. The pass is good, zooming into the hands of a Dolphins teammate! Since 1983, Miami Dolphins quarterback Dan Marino has made plays like this one look easy. In 1995, the man wearing the number thirteen on his uniform started breaking **career** (kuh-reer) National Football League, or NFL, records for most passes completed and most yards gained in passing. After thirteen **professional** (pro-FESH-un-ul) seasons, Dan's passes had sent **receivers** (ree-SEE-verz) running 48,841 yards across football fields. That's almost 21 miles!

◀ Dan is famous for his great passes.

5

Baseball Calls

Dan Marino was born in Pittsburgh, Pennsylvania, on September 15, 1961. Dan always loved sports. And his family helped him play as much as possible. His dad worked nights, but he coached Dan's Little League team.

He also spent many afternoons playing catch with his son. Dan's grandfather lived only a few blocks away, next to Pittsburgh Pirates baseball star Willie Stargell. Willie sometimes played **wiffle ball** (WIHF-ul ball) with young Dan. In high school, Dan starred as shortstop and pitcher. Baseball's Kansas City Royals tried to **sign** (SYN) Dan, but he wanted to play a different sport.

Willie Stargell

Many boys who play in Little League dream of becoming baseball stars. But Dan had another sport in mind. ▶

6

Finding Football

Dan began playing in tackle football **leagues** (LEEGZ) in fourth grade. He always played quarterback. By his senior year in high school, Dan also started as punter and placekicker. But his best work was as a quarterback. He threw sixteen touchdown passes that season.

One reason Dan decided not to play baseball with the Royals was because he wanted to attend college. He received a **scholarship** (SKOL-ur-ship) to play football for his hometown school, the University of Pittsburgh. The school was called "Pitt" and the team was called the Panthers. As a star football player, Dan was a local hero.

◀ Dan was good at many sports, but football was his favorite.

9

Pitt Is It

Even before his first game, Dan was big news at college. He grew up in Pittsburgh, and was playing for the hometown school. In the middle of his first year, Dan earned the position of starting quarterback. The team finished with eleven wins and one loss. Dan led his team to four bowl games, or post-season games, in four seasons. Each bowl game was on television, so people across the country watched Dan play. When Dan finished college, Pitt **retired** (re-TYRD) his **jersey** (JER-zee) number. No player at Pitt could ever wear number thirteen again.

People across the country watched Dan play for the Pitt Panthers. ▶

Welcome to Florida

The Miami Dolphins used its first pick in the 1983 college **draft** (DRAFT) to choose Dan. As a first-round choice, and as quarterback, fans and reporters thought Dan should be a star right away. He started only nine games that year, but he threw twenty touchdown passes. Dan helped the Dolphins get to the playoffs. In his second season, Dan played like a **veteran** (VET-er-un). He tossed 48 touchdown passes, the highest number in his career. Dan added another 1,001 yards to his total in the three playoff games that the Dolphins played in 1984. This passer from Pittsburgh gave the Dolphins its first **conference** (KON-frents) title in more than ten years.

◀ Dan quickly proved that he was a great first pick for the Dolphins in the 1983 draft.

13

On to the Super Bowl

The Dolphins won the American Football Conference (AFC) in 1984. They went on to play the winners of the National Football Conference (NFC), the San Francisco 49ers, in Super Bowl XIX (19) on January 20, 1985. But the Dolphins lost, with a score of 38 to 16. More than ten years later, Dan would still be waiting for a chance to do better and earn a Super Bowl winner's ring. For the first four years after the Super Bowl, the Dolphins couldn't even win enough games to get back to the playoffs, let alone to the Super Bowl.

Dan's passes were enough to help get the Dolphins to the Super Bowl in the 1984 season. But they weren't enough to win it. ▶

Wanting a Winner

Dan's great passes alone couldn't make the Dolphins into **champions** (CHAM-pee-unz). Fans remembered how the Dolphins had won two Super Bowls in 1972 and 1973. They wanted Dan to help the team win more Super Bowls. At Dolphins games, some fans would boo Dan for making mistakes. Because quarterbacks are in charge of calling plays, Dan has been blamed for bad plays or mistakes more than other players on the team. When fans think of Dan's career, some think of his great passes. Others think that he didn't help the team win championships.

◀ Quarterbacks are often blamed for calling bad plays or making mistakes. That happens to Dan sometimes. But many fans also cheer for Dan's great passes.

Playing with Pain

Being a quarterback is a tough job. He takes a lot of tackles! At six feet, four inches tall and 224 pounds, even someone as big as Dan can get hurt. Dan played 145 games in a row before his **Achilles tendon** (ah-KIL-eez TEN-dun) was injured. He still can't stand on tiptoe because his heel never fully healed. When he plays, Dan wears a leg brace to protect his left leg. Because of this and other injuries, Dan has a small limp. But he doesn't get too upset. After five knee operations, he joked that they were his "oil changes." They help to keep him running.

18

Dan has been hurt a lot. But he still plays as hard as he can. ▶

Passing History

Dan has set more than 25 NFL records. Some are for a single season, and others are for a career. From 1984 to 1986, he became the first quarterback to throw 30 or more touchdown passes for three seasons in a row. Dan set three records in 1995. He became history's leading quarterback in passes completed, topping Fran Tarkenton's record of 3,686 completed passes. Dan became the king of career passing yards, and has thrown footballs for more than 50,000 yards. Fran Tarkenton had set the record for the most touchdowns thrown in a career—342. But Dan beat that record too!

◀ Dan has set many records. He has proven that he chose the right sport for himself when he chose to play football.

Marino the Man

While Dan was in college, he earned a **degree** (dih-GREE) studying television and radio, and how to speak well in public. He played himself in the movie *Ace Ventura: Pet Detective*, and has been in many **commercials** (kuh-MER-shulz). Fans think Dan could be a sports announcer someday. Dan has a wife named Claire, three sons, and a daughter. One of Dan's sons, Michael, has **autism** (AW-tizm). Autism is a disorder that keeps Michael from responding to others, even his family. The Dan Marino Foundation raises money to help children with problems like Michael's. As a quarterback and as a person, Dan always wants to do more.

Glossary

Achilles tendon (ah-KIL-eez TEN-dun) The part of the body that joins the lower leg muscle to the heel bone.

autism (AW-tizm) A disorder that keeps people from responding to others.

career (kuh-reer) A person's chosen work.

champion (CHAM-pee-un) The very best at something.

commercial (kuh-MER-shul) A message selling something on television or radio that is played during and between programs.

conference (KON-frents) An organization of sports teams.

degree (dih-GREE) A certificate saying that you've finished a course of study.

draft (DRAFT) A time when professional teams take turns choosing new players from colleges, high schools, and other countries.

jersey (JER-zee) In football, the shirt of a player's uniform.

league (LEEG) An organization of sports teams.

professional (pro-FESH-un-ul) Someone who is paid for his or her work.

receiver (ree-SEE-ver) Anyone meant to catch the football.

retire (re-TYR) To stop working or using something.

scholarship (SKOL-ur-ship) Money set aside to pay for a student-athlete's education once he or she has agreed to play for that school's team.

sign (SYN) Hire.

veteran (VET-er-un) A person who has a lot of experience doing something.

wiffle ball (WIHF-ul ball) A game played with a white plastic ball the size of a baseball, with holes that make the ball curve when thrown.

23

Index